MW00675218

TAKE TIME

Helpful reminders to help you have
order, balance and purpose in your life!!!

by

Marian Langston Heard

As seen with Bishop T.D. Jakes and Pastor
Paula White speaking about leadership on
the 'God's Leading Ladies' program

1

Special thanks to my family

my parents
Ural and Indiana Langston

my husband
Winlow Heard

my sons and daughters-in-law
Gregory and Denielle Pemberton Heard
Derek and Kimberly Main Heard

sisters
Patricia Bailey Williams
Phyllis Little
Gail Grant

my late brother
Joseph Edmund Langston

brothers-in-law
Ronald Little, Sr.
Ronald Grant and
The late Leroy Bailey
sister-in-law
Florence G. Langston

AND

grandchildren
Michael, Rachael, Preston and Olivia

With deep appreciation
to
Lavette Sealls
your help made all the difference

PREFACE

Most of us lead very busy lives. We're always making lists of things to do and then forget where we put the lists. We promised ourselves we would go "here or there" and never get around to going. We're watching the days go by and even simple work or household tasks aren't completed. In too many instances, "things" clutter our lives.

This book is a reminder about what is really important and gives gentle thought-provoking phrases to guide us toward the finish line.

The goal is to work toward finishing one thing each week. Just one thing. Use the pages to list your own personal details and when you've completed one thing - just one thing - congratulate yourself.

Your world will be calmer, more orderly and you will have a sense of control.

Let's get started!!!

Chapter 1

Take Time...

to start your day with a prayer for the
  blessings of life   _____
to enjoy milk and cookies   _____
to give a long hug   _____
to smile   _____
to take a ride in the country   _____
to go on a long walk   _____
to sit in a rocking chair
for a quick nap
to give to good causes
to meditate
to be polite

"*Then He said to them, Go your way, eat the fat, drink the sweet, and send portions to those for whom nothing is prepared; for this day is holy to our Lord. Do not sorrow, for the joy of the Lord is your strength.*"
Nehemiah 8:10

YOUR LIST -- -- DATE _____
TO PRAY, TO REFLECT, TO PLAN AND TO ACT:

_____

_____

_____

_____

_____

_____

_____

_____

_____

_____

_____

_____

_____

_____

_____

_____

_____

_____

Chapter 2

Take Time...

for a leisurely meal   _____

for good friends   _____

for learning a new Scripture verse   _____

to read a book   _____

to see a funny movie   _____

for a visit to the library   _____

to make a call to an old friend

to go to a special event

to finish a lollipop

"Honor your father and your mother, that your days may be long upon the land which the Lord your God is giving you."

Exodus 20:12

YOUR LIST -- -- DATE _____
TO PRAY, TO REFLECT, TO PLAN AND TO ACT:

_____

_____

_____

_____

_____

_____

_____

_____

_____

_____

_____

_____

_____

_____

Chapter 3

Take Time...

to write a friend a letter   _____

to pray with children   _____

to send a card to a shut-in   _____

to visit a friend who is ill   _____

to contact distant relatives   _____

to enjoy a garden   _____

to update your holiday list or address
    book

to say you're sorry

to organize a reunion

"The earth is the Lord's and all its fullness, the world and those who dwell within."

                        Psalm 24:1

YOUR LIST -- -- DATE _____
TO PRAY, TO REFLECT, TO PLAN AND TO ACT:

_____

_____

_____

_____

_____

_____

_____

_____

_____

_____

_____

_____

_____

_____

_____

_____

_____

_____

_____

_____

Chapter 4

Take Time...

to dance in the kitchen   _____

to take risks   _____

to say "I love you"   _____

to make your doctor's appointments   _____

to read your Bible   _____

to enjoy time with your children   _____

to play with your grandchildren

to window shop

to pop popcorn

"The streets of the city shall be full of boys and girls playing in its streets."
Zechariah 8:5

YOUR LIST -- -- DATE _____
TO PRAY, TO REFLECT, TO PLAN AND TO ACT:

_____

_____

_____

_____

_____

_____

_____

_____

_____

_____

_____

_____

_____

_____

_____

_____

_____

Chapter 5

Take Time...

to day dream   _____

to look at travel brochures   _____

to visit a new car showroom   _____

to clean out your closets   _____

to give something to charity   _____

to appreciate God's gifts   _____

to write a thank you note

to polish all your shoes

to go to a fancy restaurant - for lunch

to vote

"Therefore, my beloved and longed-for-brethren, my joy and crown, so stand fast in the Lord, beloved."

Philippians 4:1

YOUR LIST -- -- DATE _____
TO PRAY, TO REFLECT, TO PLAN AND TO ACT:

_____

_____

_____

_____

_____

_____

_____

_____

_____

_____

_____

_____

_____

_____

_____

_____

_____

_____

_____

Chapter 6

Take Time...

to clean out your wallet   _____

to check your bank statements   _____

to listen to the wind   _____

to look at the stars   _____

to visit a museum   _____

to visit an art gallery   _____

to treat yourself to a new hairstyle

to renew your driver's license

to pray for God's wisdom

"But the fruit of the Spirit is love, joy, peace, longsuffering, kindness, goodness, faithfulness."

Galatians 5:22

YOUR LIST -- -- DATE _____
TO PRAY, TO REFLECT, TO PLAN AND TO ACT:

_____

_____

_____

_____

_____

_____

_____

_____

_____

_____

_____

_____

_____

_____

_____

_____

_____

_____

Chapter 7

Take Time...

to wear red socks around the house _____

to wear a fun T-shirt _____

to sing - even if it is "off-key" _____

to pray _____

to admit you made a mistake _____

to donate clothes to a charitable _____

   organization (many of them even pick up)

to put cucumber slices on your eyes and

   rest for 10 minutes

to know that God loves you

"Fear not, for I am with you; be not dismayed, for I am your God. I will strengthen you, yes, I will help you, I will uphold you with my righteous right hand."

        Isaiah 41:10

YOUR LIST -- -- DATE _____
TO PRAY, TO REFLECT, TO PLAN AND TO ACT:

_____

_____

_____

_____

_____

_____

_____

_____

_____

_____

_____

_____

_____

_____

_____

_____

_____

Chapter 8

Take Time...

to paint   _____

to learn a craft   _____

to take care of your pet   _____

to clean out your clutter drawers   _____

to take your loose change to the bank   _____

to check the buttons and hems on your   _____

     best suits

to wash and wax your car (inside and

     out)

to put on your sneakers

to go to a Bible study class

"For of Him and through Him and to Him are all things, to whom be glory forever. Amen"

                       Romans 11:36

YOUR LIST -- -- DATE _____
TO PRAY, TO REFLECT, TO PLAN AND TO ACT:

_____

_____

_____

_____

_____

_____

_____

_____

_____

_____

_____

_____

_____

_____

_____

_____

_____

Chapter 9

Take Time...

to wear bright red polish on your toenails _____

to sing in the shower _____

to play your favorite song _____

to list God's gifts in your life _____

to store off season clothes properly _____

to buy one or two gifts to have on hand _____

to stroll down the aisles of your favorite
   drugstore (mine is CVS)

to put your insurance policies in one place

to take a ride several miles from home

"God is wise in heart and mighty in strength. Who has hardened himself
against Him and prospered?"

Job 9:4

YOUR LIST -- -- DATE _____
TO PRAY, TO REFLECT, TO PLAN AND TO ACT:

_____

_____

_____

_____

_____

_____

_____

_____

_____

_____

_____

_____

_____

_____

_____

_____

_____

_____

Chapter 10

Take Time...

to put your personal books in order   _____

to write a will   _____

to take your medicine   _____

to walk   _____

to read the daily newspaper   _____

to put old photos in an album and label   _____
   them

to take your vitamins

to order flavored coffee

to talk to God about your sins

to keep your promises

"Therefore, my beloved brethren, be steadfast, immovable, always abounding in the work of the Lord, knowing that your labor is not in vain in the Lord."
I Corinthians 15:58

YOUR LIST -- -- DATE _____
TO PRAY, TO REFLECT, TO PLAN AND TO ACT:

_____

_____

_____

_____

_____

_____

_____

_____

_____

_____

_____

_____

_____

_____

_____

_____

_____

_____

_____

Chapter 11

Take Time...

to eat by candlelight   _____

to have BIG dreams   _____

to get your annual physical   _____

to pray for strength   _____

to toast special occasions   _____

to have bottled water stored away   _____

to go to a ball game and cheer very loudly

to own and use some pretty stationery

to celebrate accomplishments

"Great is our Lord, and mighty in power; His understanding is infinite."
Psalm 147:5

YOUR LIST -- -- DATE _____
TO PRAY, TO REFLECT, TO PLAN AND TO ACT:

_____

_____

_____

_____

_____

_____

_____

_____

_____

_____

_____

_____

_____

_____

_____

_____

_____

_____

_____

Chapter 12

Take Time...

to rest before special events   _____

to turn your mattress   _____

to celebrate with family and friends   _____

to own a pair of "pretty" shoes   _____

to smile at God's goodness   _____

to have at least two birthday parties   _____
    each year (one at home - one in "a
    wonderful place")

to think about planning the elements of
    your funeral

to buy a lace handkerchief

to spend a day alone

"That the Lord, your God may show us the way in which we should walk and
the things we should do."
Jeremiah 42:3

YOUR LIST -- -- DATE _____
TO PRAY, TO REFLECT, TO PLAN AND TO ACT:

_____

_____

_____

_____

_____

_____

_____

_____

_____

_____

_____

_____

_____

_____

_____

_____

_____

_____

_____

_____

Chapter 13

Take Time...

to disinfect your telephones   _____

to take lots of pictures   _____

to treat yourself to a great perfume   _____

to take a great vacation with your family _____

to become an expert in something   _____

to organize a Bible study group   _____

to air out your home

to really celebrate wedding anniversaries

to rest during the day

"For the kingdom is the Lord's, and He rules over the nations."
                                            Psalm 22:28

YOUR LIST -- -- DATE _____
TO PRAY, TO REFLECT, TO PLAN AND TO ACT:

_____

_____

_____

_____

_____

_____

_____

_____

_____

_____

_____

_____

_____

_____

_____

_____

_____

_____

Chapter 14

Take Time...

to disinfect your doorknobs   _____

to have a supply of batteries   _____

to have a pizza party   _____

to order some engraved note cards   _____

to know your neighbors   _____

to tell loved ones where you keep   _____

    important papers

to pray for your children

to learn the names of elected leaders of

    your state

to support your spouse

"He who gets wisdom loves his own soul; he who keeps understanding will find good."

                 Proverbs 19:8

YOUR LIST -- -- DATE _____
TO PRAY, TO REFLECT, TO PLAN AND TO ACT:

_____

_____

_____

_____

_____

_____

_____

_____

_____

_____

_____

_____

_____

_____

_____

_____

_____

Chapter 15

Take Time...

to tell loved ones your wishes regarding   _____

   your final resting place   _____

to go to the circus   _____

to spend time with people who love you   _____

to use a date book   _____

to organize your holiday decorations   _____

to tell people you love them

to have a pot luck supper

to thank God every day

to write your favorite recipes for

   family members

Jesus answered and said to him, "most assuredly, I say to you, unless one is born again, he cannot see the Kingdom of God."

                                     John 3:3

YOUR LIST -- -- DATE _____
TO PRAY, TO REFLECT, TO PLAN AND TO ACT:

_____

_____

_____

_____

_____

_____

_____

_____

_____

_____

_____

_____

_____

_____

_____

_____

Chapter 16

Take Time...

to read   _____

to have a calendar handy   _____

to try a new recipe   _____

to learn how to make a short speech   _____

to spend time with people you love   _____

to put things in their proper place   _____

to appreciate your blessings

to go to a play or musical event

to go to a zoo

"Cast your burden on the Lord, and He shall sustain you; He shall never permit the righteous to be moved."

Psalm 55:22

YOUR LIST -- -- DATE _____
TO PRAY, TO REFLECT, TO PLAN AND TO ACT:

Chapter 17

Take Time...

to learn how to really explore the Internet _____

to make a "to do" list and finish it   _____

to tell people you appreciate them   _____

to acknowledge your blessings   _____

to remove clutter   _____

to invite friends over to see your favorite   _____
  movie

to slow down when you face adversity

to have a pad and pen handy

"And now, my daughter, do not fear; I will do for you all that you request,
for all the people of my town know that you are a virtuous woman."
                                                      Ruth 3:11

YOUR LIST -- -- DATE _____
TO PRAY, TO REFLECT, TO PLAN AND TO ACT:

_____

_____

_____

_____

_____

_____

_____

_____

_____

_____

_____

_____

_____

_____

_____

_____

_____

_____

_____

Chapter 18

Take Time...

to host a theme or costume party   _____

to say thank you - a lot   _____

to pray for peace   _____

to give thanks for your blessings   _____

to learn to take a great photograph   _____

to tell someone how important they   _____

   are in your life

to browse in a second-hand store

to congratulate yourself

to attend a school play

"So you shall serve the Lord your God, and He will bless your bread and your water. And I will take sickness away from the midst of you."

Exodus 23:25

YOUR LIST -- -- DATE _____
TO PRAY, TO REFLECT, TO PLAN AND TO ACT:

_____

_____

_____

_____

_____

_____

_____

_____

_____

_____

_____

_____

_____

_____

_____

_____

_____

_____

_____

Chapter 19

Take Time...

to read all night	_____
to visit the dentist regularly	_____
to fast	_____
to walk on a beach	_____
to carve a pumpkin	_____
to drive through a covered bridge	_____
to enjoy a scoop of ice cream	
to watch TV all night	
to worship with shut-ins	
to check your smoke detectors	
(or install smoke detectors)	

"The Lord is good, a strong hold in the day of trouble; and He knows those who trust Him."

                        Nahum 1:7

YOUR LIST -- -- DATE _____
TO PRAY, TO REFLECT, TO PLAN AND TO ACT:

_____

_____

_____

_____

_____

_____

_____

_____

_____

_____

_____

_____

_____

_____

_____

_____

_____

Chapter 20

Take Time...

to go to the worship place of your
   choice

to sit by the water

to learn to communicate more clearly

to every now and then - eat a hot dog

to visit an antique shop

to learn how to kneel and get up
   gracefully

to get your facts straight

to learn how to negotiate

to introduce people

"My foot has held fast to His steps; I have kept His way and not turned
aside."

        Job 23:11

YOUR LIST -- -- DATE _____
TO PRAY, TO REFLECT, TO PLAN AND TO ACT:

_____

_____

_____

_____

_____

_____

_____

_____

_____

_____

_____

_____

_____

_____

_____

_____

_____

Chapter 21

Take Time...

to get 20 minutes of sun - and don't forget

    the sunscreen   _____

to write down your goals   _____

to play videos all night   _____

to change your toothbrush   _____

to tell yourself that you are fabulous _____

to pray for good health   _____

to go to a book signing

to get your eyes examined

to sharpen your pencils

"But without faith it is impossible to please Him, for he who comes to God must believe that He is, and that He is a rewarder of those who diligently seek Him."

                Hebrews 11:6

YOUR LIST -- -- DATE _____
TO PRAY, TO REFLECT, TO PLAN AND TO ACT:

_____

_____

_____

_____

_____

_____

_____

_____

_____

_____

_____

_____

_____

_____

_____

_____

_____

Chapter 22

Take Time...

to borrow free videos from your library	_____
to get tested for diabetes	_____
to remember life is not fair	_____
to consider His blessings in your family	_____
to clean out your medicine cabinet	_____
to shop for bargains	_____

for soaking in a hot tub

to sign up for free stuff

to repair broken relationships

"He also opens their ear to instruction, and commands that they turn from iniquity."
        Job 36:10

YOUR LIST -- -- DATE _____
TO PRAY, TO REFLECT, TO PLAN AND TO ACT:

_____

_____

_____

_____

_____

_____

_____

_____

_____

_____

_____

_____

_____

_____

_____

_____

_____

_____

Chapter 23

Take Time...

to write clearer and neater _____

to go to a graduation celebration _____

to soak your feet _____

to read to a child _____

to finish a 500 piece puzzle _____

to volunteer _____

to water your plants

to put cream on your elbows

to thank God for your friends

"May the Lord our God be with us, as He was with our fathers. May He not leave us nor forsake us."
                    I Kings 8:57

YOUR LIST -- -- DATE _____
TO PRAY, TO REFLECT, TO PLAN AND TO ACT:

_____

_____

_____

_____

_____

_____

_____

_____

_____

_____

_____

_____

_____

_____

_____

_____

_____

_____

Chapter 24

Take Time...

to put all the candles on your
   birthday cake

to file your taxes on time

to review your diet

to let your family know you love them

to appreciate every sunrise

to give soup and tuna to your local
   food bank

to put a lot of cream on your hands
   twice a day and at night

to tie your shoe laces

to tie a child's shoe laces

"So rend your heart, and not your garments; return to the Lord your God, for He is gracious and merciful, slow to anger, and of great kindness; and He relents from doing harm."

Joel 2:13

YOUR LIST -- -- DATE _____
TO PRAY, TO REFLECT, TO PLAN AND TO ACT:

_____

_____

_____

_____

_____

_____

_____

_____

_____

_____

_____

_____

_____

_____

_____

_____

_____

_____

Chapter 25

Take Time...

to be able to discuss sports _____

to go swimming _____

to pay off your student loans _____

to walk in a beautiful place _____

to change your linen twice a week _____

to say you're wonderful and thank God _____

  for a great attitude

to stop smoking

(for all the males in your life) to check

  their prostate numbers

to appreciate every sunset

"Many, O Lord my God, are your wonderful works which you have done; and your thoughts toward us cannot be recounted to you in order; if I would declare and speak to them, they are more than can be numbered."

Psalms 40:5

YOUR LIST -- -- DATE _____
TO PRAY, TO REFLECT, TO PLAN AND TO ACT:

_____

_____

_____

_____

_____

_____

_____

_____

_____

_____

_____

_____

_____

_____

_____

_____

_____

_____

_____

_____

_____

_____

Chapter 26

Take Time...

to take a mental health day   _____

to keep gas in your car   _____

to own a fire retardant chest or safe   _____

to visit New York or another large city   _____

to eat on your best dishes   _____

to buy fresh flowers once a month   _____

to understand the challenges God has

   helped you to overcome

to save your money

to learn the rules of one major sport

"To stand every morning to thank and praise the Lord, and likewise at evening."
                   I Chronicles 23:30

YOUR LIST -- -- DATE _____
TO PRAY, TO REFLECT, TO PLAN AND TO ACT:

_____

_____

_____

_____

_____

_____

_____

_____

_____

_____

_____

_____

_____

_____

_____

_____

_____

_____

_____

_____

Chapter 27

Take Time...

to take half your vacation time in   _____

   single days - if possible   _____

to turn your furniture cushions   _____

to wear your favorite color   _____

to turn your problems over to God   _____

to treat yourself to a day off   _____

to eat a bowl of soup

to take your cans and bottles to the

   recycle center

to be aware of your surroundings

to focus

"Out of heaven He let you hear His voice, that He might instruct you; on earth He showed you His great fire, and you heard His words out of the midst of the fire."

                                  Deuteronomy 4:36

YOUR LIST -- -- DATE _____
TO PRAY, TO REFLECT, TO PLAN AND TO ACT:

_____

_____

_____

_____

_____

_____

_____

_____

_____

_____

_____

_____

_____

_____

_____

_____

_____

_____

_____

_____

Chapter 28

Take Time...

to buy U.S. savings bonds   _____

to learn some new funny jokes   _____

to call an old friend   _____

to let others know God is in your life   _____

to water your plants   _____

to remember the special occasions   _____

  for others

to go to a special brunch

to be flexible and appreciate the

  opinions of others

"Be anxious for nothing, but in everything by prayer and supplication, with
thanksgiving, let your requests be made known to God."
Philippians 4:6

YOUR LIST -- -- DATE _____
TO PRAY, TO REFLECT, TO PLAN AND TO ACT:

_____

_____

_____

_____

_____

_____

_____

_____

_____

_____

_____

_____

_____

_____

_____

_____

_____

_____

_____

Chapter 29

Take Time...

to be a vegetarian for a week   _____

to pay your bills on time   _____

to tell someone where you're going   _____

to know an alternate route home   _____

to rest and reflect   _____

to write to your representative in   _____

   Congress

to sing in the choir

to explore a new museum

to stay involved

"The Lord is my strength and song, and He has become my salvation."
                                             Psalm 118:14

YOUR LIST -- -- DATE _____
TO PRAY, TO REFLECT, TO PLAN AND TO ACT:

_____

_____

_____

_____

_____

_____

_____

_____

_____

_____

_____

_____

_____

_____

_____

_____

_____

_____

_____

Chapter 30

Take Time...

to visit your neighbors   _____

to have a quiet place to meditate   _____

to save more money   _____

to keep stamps on hand   _____

to review your debts   _____

to review your budget   _____

to know your net worth

to have a 3-5 year plan

to get up when you wake up - no

   alarm clock

"A man who has friends must himself be friendly, but there is a friend who sticks closer than a brother."

Proverbs 18:24

YOUR LIST -- -- DATE _____
TO PRAY, TO REFLECT, TO PLAN AND TO ACT:

_____

_____

_____

_____

_____

_____

_____

_____

_____

_____

_____

_____

_____

_____

_____

_____

_____

_____

Chapter 31

Take Time...

to soak your feet in a great fragrance

   or oil _____

to review your life insurance _____

to stay active _____

to listen to uplifting music _____

to be happy _____

to nap _____

to ask God for forgiveness

to re-invest your dividends

to write to the President

"Now may the God of patience and comfort grant you to be likeminded toward one another, according to Christ Jesus."

Romans 15:5

YOUR LIST -- -- DATE _____
TO PRAY, TO REFLECT, TO PLAN AND TO ACT:

_____

_____

_____

_____

_____

_____

_____

_____

_____

_____

_____

_____

_____

_____

_____

_____

_____

_____

Chapter 32

Take Time...

to watch a child play a game and

   cheer loudly   _____

to listen to God's instructions   _____

to remember the good times   _____

to encourage a child   _____

to keep a journal   _____

to write your obituary   _____

to forget the bad times

to always carry identification

to take a boat ride

Then he said to them, "Go your way, eat the fat, drink the sweet, and send portions to those for whom nothing is prepared; for this day is holy to our Lord. Do not sorrow, for the joy of the Lord is your strength."

Nehemiah 8:10

YOUR LIST -- -- DATE _____
TO PRAY, TO REFLECT, TO PLAN AND TO ACT:

_____

_____

_____

_____

_____

_____

_____

_____

_____

_____

_____

_____

_____

_____

_____

_____

_____

_____

Chapter 33

Take Time...

to go to church in the evening   _____

to learn great table manners   _____

to listen to the wind   _____

to forgive and forget   _____

to give someone a compliment   _____

to visit a farm   _____

to enjoy the moment

to ask God for guidance

to clean your dryer filter

"For the Lord God is a sun and shield; the Lord will give grace and glory; no good thing will He withhold from those who walk uprightly."

                                            Psalm 84:11

YOUR LIST -- -- DATE _____
TO PRAY, TO REFLECT, TO PLAN AND TO ACT:

_____

_____

_____

_____

_____

_____

_____

_____

_____

_____

_____

_____

_____

_____

_____

_____

_____

_____

Chapter 34

Take Time...

to save for tomorrow   _____

to kneel in prayer   _____

to enjoy visiting a park   _____

to sing   _____

to have an ice cream sundae party   _____

to make a great soup   _____

to say "ask" not ax

to say thank you - often

to clean out your old pocketbook
  (or briefcase)

"Fear not, O land; be glad and rejoice, for the Lord has done marvelous things!"
                    Joel 2:21

YOUR LIST -- -- DATE _____
TO PRAY, TO REFLECT, TO PLAN AND TO ACT:

_____

_____

_____

_____

_____

_____

_____

_____

_____

_____

_____

_____

_____

_____

_____

_____

_____

_____

Chapter 35

Take Time...

to return phone calls	_____
to go to the movies	_____
to pray before meals	_____
to install a carbon monoxide detector	_____
to check your cholesterol	_____
to close your eyes and rest	_____
to play your favorite songs/music	
to go to a seminar	
to put emergency numbers near the phone	

"If any of you lacks wisdom, let him ask of God, who gives to all liberally and without reproach, and it will be given to him."

James 1:5

YOUR LIST-- -- DATE _____
TO PRAY, TO REFLECT, TO PLAN AND TO ACT:

_____

_____

_____

_____

_____

_____

_____

_____

_____

_____

_____

_____

_____

_____

_____

_____

_____

_____

_____

_____

_____

Chapter 36

Take Time...

to enjoy today and thank God for
  today's joy   _____

to meet new people   _____

to have a bar-be-que   _____

to visit a great perfume counter   _____

to pay your parking ticket   _____

to keep in touch with old friends   _____

to buy flowers for yourself

to buy a good lotion

to remember "the glass is not half full," -
  it's overflowing

"And if it seems evil to you to serve the Lord, choose for yourself this day
whom you will serve; whether the gods which your fathers served that were
on the other side of the river, or the gods of the Amorites, in whose land you
dwell. But as for me and my house, we will serve the Lord."

Joshua 24:15

YOUR LIST -- -- DATE _____
TO PRAY, TO REFLECT, TO PLAN AND TO ACT:

_____

_____

_____

_____

_____

_____

_____

_____

_____

_____

_____

_____

_____

_____

_____

_____

_____

_____

_____

Chapter 37

Take Time...

to save for a great vacation   _____

to give a child your time   _____

to listen   _____

to invite your neighbors for a visit   _____

to ask your doctor about an aspirin a day _____

to understand the expectations of those   _____

   you work with and for

to become an expert at something

to be courteous to those who wait on you

to plan your day with God in mind

"Call onto me, and I will answer thee, and show you great and mighty things, which you do not know."

Jeremiah 33:3

YOUR LIST -- -- DATE _____
TO PRAY, TO REFLECT, TO PLAN AND TO ACT:

_____

_____

_____

_____

_____

_____

_____

_____

_____

_____

_____

_____

_____

_____

_____

_____

_____

_____

Chapter 38

Take Time...

to congratulate and encourage others
   as God would have us to do   _____

to laugh at absolutely nothing at all   _____

to keep a battery-powered radio handy _____

to follow school bus signals   _____

to get a hair cut   _____

to plan and act - if you wait for the   _____
   "perfect time" most likely you won't act

to teach a child how to read

to have a smoke detector (and check the
   batteries)

to obey speed limits

"Behold, God is mighty, but despises no one; He is mighty in strength of understanding."
                      Job 36:5

YOUR LIST -- -- DATE _____
TO PRAY, TO REFLECT, TO PLAN AND TO ACT:

_____

_____

_____

_____

_____

_____

_____

_____

_____

_____

_____

_____

_____

_____

_____

_____

_____

_____

_____

_____

Chapter 39

Take Time...

to spend time with those you love and

those who love you   _____

to tutor a child   _____

to inventory your possessions   _____

to tend to a plant and watch over it   _____

to take your vitamins   _____

to tell someone where you keep your   _____

important papers

to keep a picture of any valuables in a

safety deposit box

to complete a will

to share your love of God with friends

And He said to them, "Go into all the world and preach the gospel to every creature."
        Mark 16:15

YOUR LIST -- -- DATE _____
TO PRAY, TO REFLECT, TO PLAN AND TO ACT:

Chapter 40

Take Time...

to plan ahead so you're always on time _____

to put copies of your taxes in a safe place _____

to celebrate your favorite holiday _____

to enjoy an outdoor concert _____

to wash your hands - often _____

to plan a budget and live within your _____

   means and ask God to guide you

to check your hems, buttons and collars

to sit up straight

to make sure all area rugs are "trip proof"

"And now abide faith, hope, love, these three; but the greatest of these is love."

    I Corinthians 13:13

YOUR LIST -- -- DATE _____
TO PRAY, TO REFLECT, TO PLAN AND TO ACT:

_____

_____

_____

_____

_____

_____

_____

_____

_____

_____

_____

_____

_____

_____

_____

_____

_____

_____

Chapter 41

Take Time...

to learn how to write a great letter   _____

to learn how to operate a computer   _____

to clean your refrigerator   _____

to donate food to the poor   _____

to keep up with the news   _____

to walk with purpose   _____

to do things that would make your
   mother proud

to forgive yourself as God would forgive
   you

to keep your stairs well lighted

"I will praise You, O Lord, with my whole heart; I will tell of all your marvelous works.

Psalm 9:1

YOUR LIST -- -- DATE _____
TO PRAY, TO REFLECT, TO PLAN AND TO ACT:

_____

_____

_____

_____

_____

_____

_____

_____

_____

_____

_____

_____

_____

_____

_____

_____

_____

Chapter 42

Take Time...

to practice having a firm (but not too
 firm) handshake   _____

to watch your favorite TV program   _____

to brush and floss   _____

to feed the birds   _____

to acknowledge your gifts   _____

to remember what's really important in   _____
 your life (and use this page to start
 your list)

to practice something you're interested
 in enhancing

to know that God loves you

"Bless the Lord, O my soul; and all that is within me, bless His holy name."
Psalms 103:1

YOUR LIST -- -- DATE _____
TO PRAY, TO REFLECT, TO PLAN AND TO ACT:

_____

_____

_____

_____

_____

_____

_____

_____

_____

_____

_____

_____

_____

_____

_____

_____

_____

_____

_____

Chapter 43

Take Time...

to write down your goals (use this space

   to start your list)   _____

to make a rock garden   _____

to spend a day with a child   _____

to know your blood sugar levels _____

to neaten your room   _____

to review your progress and thank God _____

   for supporting your plan

to clean your glasses and put them in the

   same place

to buy some good luggage

to appreciate each moment

"Trust in the Lord with all your heart, and lean not on your own under-standing."
                          Proverbs 3:5

YOUR LIST -- -- DATE _____
TO PRAY, TO REFLECT, TO PLAN AND TO ACT:

_____

_____

_____

_____

_____

_____

_____

_____

_____

_____

_____

_____

_____

_____

_____

_____

_____

_____

_____

_____

Chapter 44

Take Time...

to find a favorite walking path   _____

to hold an infant   _____

to be obedient   _____

to savor a biscotti   _____

to visit a bird sanctuary   _____

to visit your family   _____

to turn off your cell phone

to study a world map

to listen to scripture tapes

"Her ways are ways of pleasantness, and all her paths are peace."
Proverbs 3:17

YOUR LIST -- -- DATE _____
TO PRAY, TO REFLECT, TO PLAN AND TO ACT:

_____

_____

_____

_____

_____

_____

_____

_____

_____

_____

_____

_____

_____

_____

_____

_____

_____

_____

_____

_____

_____

Chapter 45

Take Time...

to finish your big projects (list the

    BIG projects on this page)   _____

to make special holiday calls   _____

to ask God's direction in making peace   _____

to buy a pair of snazzy boots   _____

to finish one thing today   _____

to pray for others   _____

to express your gratitude

to drink more water

to list impossible things that you want

    to do - then try just one (use the space

    on the next page)

"We love Him because He first loved us."

I John 4:19

YOUR LIST -- -- DATE _____
TO PRAY, TO REFLECT, TO PLAN AND TO ACT:

_____

_____

_____

_____

_____

_____

_____

_____

_____

_____

_____

_____

_____

_____

_____

_____

_____

_____

Chapter 46

Take Time...

to call on Jesus   _____

to feed some ducks   _____

to confirm your strengths   _____

to work on your challenges   _____

to condense your message   _____

to get a day pass for a great health club   _____

to negotiate what you want

to treasure your friends

to plan a family picnic

"To speak evil of no one, to be peaceable, gentle, showing all humility to all men."

      Titus 3:2

YOUR LIST -- -- DATE _____
TO PRAY, TO REFLECT, TO PLAN AND TO ACT:

_____

_____

_____

_____

_____

_____

_____

_____

_____

_____

_____

_____

_____

_____

_____

_____

_____

_____

_____

Chapter 47

Take Time...

to thank the friends who treasure you   _____

to organize your recipes   _____

to sit and eat   _____

to encourage family worship   _____

to get a piggy bank   _____

to organize a family reunion   _____

to host your spriitual leader to a family
  dinner

to know your family's history

to update your address book

"But let all those rejoice who put their trust in You; let them ever shout for
joy, because You defend them; let those also who love Your name be joyful in
You."
     Psalm 5:11

YOUR LIST -- -- DATE _____
TO PRAY, TO REFLECT, TO PLAN AND TO ACT:

_____

_____

_____

_____

_____

_____

_____

_____

_____

_____

_____

_____

_____

_____

_____

_____

_____

_____

_____

Chapter 48

Take Time...

to dry some flowers   _____

to do it now   _____

to change your light bulbs   _____

to plant some flowers   _____

to sit and watch people   _____

to laugh out loud   _____

to go for a free make up session at the
mall

to browse in a bookstore

to enjoy God's gift of nature and the
seasons

"The Lord is my strength and song, and He has become my salvation."
Psalm 118:14

YOUR LIST -- -- DATE _____
TO PRAY, TO REFLECT, TO PLAN AND TO ACT:

_____

_____

_____

_____

_____

_____

_____

_____

_____

_____

_____

_____

_____

_____

_____

_____

_____

_____

Chapter 49

Take Time...

to blow bubbles   _____

to attend a reunion   _____

to build a fire and roast marshmallows   _____

to practice writing well   _____

to visit a nursing home   _____

to test drive a new car   _____

to try a new lipstick

to ride a bus to the end of the line

to help clean up a vacant lot

"But the Lord is in His holy temple. Let all the earth keep silence before Him."
    Habakkuk 2:20

YOUR LIST -- -- DATE _____
TO PRAY, TO REFLECT, TO PLAN AND TO ACT:

_____

_____

_____

_____

_____

_____

_____

_____

_____

_____

_____

_____

_____

_____

_____

_____

_____

_____

_____

_____

Chapter 50

Take Time...

to have a picnic with your friends   _____

to deliver a plant to a senior citizen   _____

to close your eyes and rest right now   _____

to plan your dream trip   _____

to go to dinner with a good friend   _____

to buy a great reading lamp   _____

to have a sanctuary/quiet place in your
  home

to use a night light

to smile at a stranger and share God's
  love

"Inasmuch as there is none like you, O Lord, (You are great, and Your name is great in might)."
Jeremiah 10:6

YOUR LIST -- -- DATE _____
TO PRAY, TO REFLECT, TO PLAN AND TO ACT:

_____

_____

_____

_____

_____

_____

_____

_____

_____

_____

_____

_____

_____

_____

_____

_____

_____

_____

_____

_____

_____

Chapter 51

Take Time...

to make potpourri	_____
to ask for an upgrade at every hotel	_____
to clean your attic	_____
to clean your basement	_____
to put a blanket in your car	_____
to mark all the birthdays/anniversaries	_____
on the calendar	
to put an umbrella in your car/case	
to ask God to give you calmness everyday	
to meet new people and try to remember	
their names	

"But seek the kingdom of God, and all these things shall be added to you. Do not fear, little flock, for it is your Father's good pleasure to give you the king-dom."

                          Luke 12:31-32

YOUR LIST -- -- DATE _____
TO PRAY, TO REFLECT, TO PLAN AND TO ACT:

_____

_____

_____

_____

_____

_____

_____

_____

_____

_____

_____

_____

_____

_____

_____

_____

_____

_____

_____

_____

_____

Chapter 52

Take Time...

to sleep in God's love _____

to take your blood pressure _____

to say thank you _____

to tour your city or town _____

to know God loves you _____

to take better care of yourself _____

to give yourself credit

to end your day with a prayer of
    thanksgiving

"Beloved, if God so loved us, we also ought to love one another.
                                                        I John 4:11

"Great mercy, and peace will be with you from God the Father and from the
Lord Jesus Christ, the Son the Father, in truth and love."
                                                        II John 1:3

"Beloved, I pray that you may prosper in all things and be in health, just as
your soul prospers."
                                                        III John 1:2

YOUR LIST -- -- DATE _____
TO PRAY, TO REFLECT, TO PLAN AND TO ACT:

_____

_____

_____

_____

_____

_____

_____

_____

_____

_____

_____

_____

_____

_____

_____

_____

_____

_____

_____

Acknowledgements

To these great friends - most of whom danced at our wedding.

Great Connecticut friends of over 50 years:

The SSL's and high school friends
Kathy Clark and Jack
Carolyn Thorne *
Joan Gallos
Kathleen "Corky" Greene
Nancy Murray
Eve Smith and Brian
Jackie and Richie Jankura
Gail Lupariello
Judy Curran
Arlene Brandenberg and Gene
Evelyn Thayer and Mike
Annette Cullen and Irv
Rosemary Lankton and Jack
Judy A. Solo
Ann Roviello
Carolyn Martin
Frannie Wadeka
Mary Sandburg and Bruce
Natalie Siavrakas and Mike
　　　AND
Carol Ciraulo from the 5th grade and Joe

AND

Other very special friends of over 40 years:

Margaret "Pickles" and Bobby McIntosh
Rita and Melvin Hayes

Suzy and Bobby Long
Marlene and Peter George
Midgie and Chris Tavares
Martha and Kenny Tavares
Hazel and George McNair
Anna and Doris* Mellow
Terri Thompson and Silvino "Val" Valeriano
Beverly Lewis
Jim and Anna Christie
Mary and Earl Mellow

From College - Two Great Friends

Juliette Bethea

Great Friend and Pen Pal Extraordinaire

Jane Zanardi and her husband, Peter
(we have exchanged weekly letters since 1963)

——————————————

*Deceased

Daniel Dennis, Sr., CPA (and spouse Mary)+
Sandra M. Edgerley (and spouse Paul)+
Russell L. Epker
Thomas G. Flynn
Charles Gifford (and spouse Anne)+
Richard Gilman
Paul S. Grogan
John P. Hamill (and spouse Katheryn)+
Raymond A. Hammond, MD,
Carolyn Golden Hebsgaard

+Dinner hosts for the Heards
and/or the United Way

A BIG DREAM REALIZED
The Millennium Fund for Children and Families
We celebrate the completion of a $30,000,000 Fund, almost a year
ahead of schedule. To those whose support and dedication to others has and will
continue to make the greater Boston community a safer
and better place for poor children and their families.
Thank you for making a big dream come true!!!

FleetBoston Financial	NSTAR
Mr. Edmund N. Ansin	Mark E. Nunnelly and Denise Dupré
osh and Anita Bekenstein	Tom and Carol O'Donnell
Mr.* and Mrs. William F. Connell	David R. and Muriel K. Pokross
Martha H. W. Crowninshield	Ben and Kate Taylor
cott and Laurie Schoen	Bill and Jane Van Faasen
tate Street Corporation	Wellington Management Company, LLP
ff and Penny Vinik	The Stride Rite Corporation
arlene and Jerry Jordan	Ted and Joan Benard-Cutler
tizens Financial Group	Mr. and Mrs. John P. Hamill
berty Mutual Group	Marian and Winlow Heard and Family
d and Lori King Rohda	Howard and Michele Kessler
an C. Tempel	Mr. and Mrs. Jonathan O. Lee
nes and Jane Wilson	Mr. and Mrs. Caleb Loring, Jr
Hunter and Pamela T. Boll	Tom and Donna May
'S Corporation	Ms. Gail McGovern
ul and Sandy Edgerley	Marie and Paul O'Brien
ssell L. Epker and Ann E. Percival	Paul F. and Elizabeth A. Quirk
n and Corinne Ferguson and family	Steve and Robin Scari
Goldberg Family Foundation	Phyllis Yale and Tucker Taft
ol, Avram, Deborah and	John R. and Margaret B. Towers
Joshua Goldberg, Trustees	Abrams Family Charitable Trust
ry and Beth Greenberg	Leo and Susan Breitman
and Mrs. Robert K. Kraft	Mr. and Mrs. Peter A. Brooke
garete E. and John A. McNeice, Jr.	Kevin and Julie Callaghan
and Nancy Shepherd	Beth and Linzee Coolidge

Mr. and Mrs. Norman Silverman
David A. Spina and Stephanie H. Spina
Mr. and Mrs. Peter S. Voss
Mr. Robert L. Beal
Blue Cross Blue Shield of Massachusetts
Ami K. and William A. Danoff
Hilary and Chris Gabrieli
The Harbert Family
Mr. and Mrs. J. Atwood Ives
Jonathan and Jeanne Lavine
Diane and Nick Lopardo
Carolyn and Peter S. Lynch
Cathy E. Minehan and
       E. Gerald Corrigan
Mr. and Mrs. William L. Saltonstall
Mr. and Mrs. John Lowell
Jane and Thomas Martin
Dorick and Priscilla Mauro
Susan Higginson McVeigh
Dr. Elsa Nunez and Dr. Richard Freeland
Diane and Deval Patrick
Peter and Suzanne Read
Mrs. Paton R. Roberts
The Estate of Seymour Rothchild
Carl and Fay Simons Family
Micho and Bill Spring
Lenore E. Tagerman
Albert and Judith Zabin
Kathleen A. Casavant
Maria Helena DaSilva
Barbara Jentis
William and Cynthia Marcus
Charlotte B. Read
Sheldon and Roberta Schoen
Juanita and Kenneth Wade
Andrew and Bliss Austin Spooner

Mary and Dan Dennis
Deanna and Tony DiNovi
John R. and Meri P. Grumbacher
Ira and Martha Jackson
Roger and Dawn Kafker
Mr. and Mrs. Edward H. Ladd
Mr. and Mrs. George M. Lovejoy, Jr.
Robert and Kathleen Mahoney
Chester R. and Joyce C. Messer
David and Lauren Murphy
William and Nancy Mutterperl
Mr. Daniel A. and Rev. Diana W. Phillips
Charlotte and Irving W. Rabb
New England Financial
Peter and Alison Small
Michael D. and Pamela K. Webb
Albert and Carol Wilson
James and Sonja Wolfsberg
Lawrence and Carol Begley
Mr. and Mrs. Robert E. Cowden, III
Gail Deegan and William Huddleston
Mr. and Mrs. Richard C. Garrison
Mr. and Mrs. Ronald A. Homer
Linda and Peter Manning
Richard A. and Helene H. Monaghan
Mr. and Mrs. Paul R. Murphy
Joseph H. Rice and Judith A. Aronstei
Sean C. Rush
Joseph and Deidre Smialowski
Edwin E. and Katharine T. Smith
Ralph and Kathleen Verni
Charlie and Steve Wagner
Michael and Rose* Zoob
Peter J. Carroll
Kathleen M. and Joseph W. Dello Rus
Mr. and Mrs. William E. Duggan

Rev. Wesley C. Blount, Jr. and Renee
Scott Blount
Patricia Brandes
Marilyn Anderson Chase
Joseph and Diane Coughlin
The Curran Family
Charles B. and Leslie E. Gordon
Matthew and Patricia Keenan
Mary Kay Leonard and Richard Valachovic
Colin and Jeanne Maclaurin
Mary Moschos
John A. Ross
Robert Sarason
Meredith L. Singer and Alan J. Chandler *in honor of their wedding*
Ray and Kelly Dunn
Andrew and Ana Flaster
Nancy C. and Arthur W. Grellier
Paul S. Grogan and Karen A. Sonnarburg
Rev. Raymond Hammond, M.D.
Rev. Gloria White-Hammond, M.D.
and the Bethel African Methodist Church
Carolyn Golden Hebsgaard
Wilbur T. and Elizabeth M. Hooven
Ted C. Johnson
Guy Lombardo
in memoriam

Michael and Barbara Eisenson
Robert J. and Marybeth Haynes
Mr. Thomas O'Neill, III
James W. and Margaret H. Perkins
Kathryn F. Plazak
Helen Chin Schlichte
Mr. and Mrs. Edwin G. Smith
Alan and Lorraine Bressler
Cheryl* and Michael Carson
Meredith and Eugene Clapp
Mr. and Mrs. Anthony T. Cope
Edith Derman
Ernest J. Dieterich

Kevin and Karen Stone
Rick Tagliaferri and Jill Mackavey
Claudia and Peter Thomas
Andrew and Annemarie Thompson

…also 10 community leaders and two staff members who wish to remain anonymous

With thanks, appreciation and admiration to:

Mayor Thomas Menino

For his extraordinary leadership and continued support for our combined efforts on behalf of children. His steadfast leadership with United Way's Success by 6 and Keeping Kids on Track initiatives have led to national award-winning efforts.

In addition, he is a partner in the After-School for All Partnership.

Thank you, Tom, for caring so deeply for others.

Thank you also for making the United Way of Massachusetts Bay the only United Way in America with its own park. On April 15, 2003, the Children's Plaza at Christopher Columbus Park, located on the Boston Harbor, was unveiled. This Plaza is dedicated to the children of Boston and all of New England and will allow them to play freely because strangers cared.

To Ed Ansin, President, WHDH-TV Boston, and President, WSVN-TV Miami,
for your extraordinary generosity in making the United Way of Massachusetts Bay the first United Way in American to have an endowed chair. I am proud to be the first recipient of the Executive Leadership Chair which cites "community leadership, innovative management, vision and determination in serving others".

Thank you, Ed, for your vision, leadership and generosity!!!
Here's another book for the plane ride!!!

Special thanks
for
advice and support
Marsha and Jack Countryman
Jason Countryman

This book reflects the "early and mostly Connecticut years."
"If your name is not here, watch for the next book."

To my benefactor,

an individual who has graciously supported the artist in me!!!

Ronald Druker

Thank you. Thank you. Thank you.

LIST THE NAME OF THOSE WHO HAVE HELPED YOU:

Leaders who have supported us "early on" and continue to help in personal and special ways:

Michele Courton Brown and Philip Brown
Frances and Bud Moseley
Liz and Ed Dugger
Josephine McNeil
Jim and Cathy Stone
Milton and Jimmy Hagins
Verniece and Isaiah Owen
John and Margarete McNiece
Howard and Michele Kessler
Nancy Korman
Carol Bolling Fulp
Jerry Martinson
Sheryl Marshall

For the Religious leaders in my life:

    *Rev. William O. Johnson, long-term Pastor of the First Baptist Church in Stratford, Connecticut

Rev. Dr. and Mrs.Michael Ellis of Columbus Avenue AME Zion Church in Boston, Massachusetts.

Evangelist Dorothy Allsop, long time family friend of Bridgeport,Connecticut

Rev. George Sanders, Presiding elder and former pastor of the Walter's Memorial AME Zion Church, Bridgeport, Connecticut

Rev. and Mrs. Timothy Howard, Walter's Memorial AME Zion Church in Bridgeport, Connecticut

Father Charles Allen, former President, Fairfield college Preparatory School, Fairfield, Connecticut

Father Aloyisious Kelly, President, Fairfield University, Fairfield, Connecticut*

---

*Deceased

To those United Way staff members who were there "at the beginning." A *very special thank you!!!*

Mike Wyman
Kevin Stone
Deloris Ford
Jeanne Black
Sara Allen
Bob Rodwell
Joe Quirk
Barbara Alexander
Dick Piccuito
Lisa Pickard
Al Hamilton
Ann Guy
Chuck Gordon
Kris Stranahan
Merle Jones Lindsay
Barbara Leonard
Don Leete
Chris O'Keeffe

Special thanks and appreciation for your support:

Pat Brandes
Renee Scott Blount
Marilyn Anderson Chase

TAKE TIME

"FEEDBACK INFORMATION"

PLEASE TAKE TIME TO WRITE AND TELL ME HOW YOU USED THIS BOOK. I WOULD LIKE TO KNOW WHAT ARE SOME OTHER THINGS YOU BELIEVE SHOULD BE ON THE "TAKE TIME" LIST.

WAS THERE ONE THING THAT ENCOURAGED YOU? CHALLENGED YOU TO ACT? REMINDED YOU ABOUT SOMETHING?

PLEASE CONTACT ME:
MARIAN L. HEARD
CHAIRMAN AND CEO
HEARD ENTERPRISES, LLC
P.O. BOX 811
NATICK, MASS. 01760

e-mail: wmheard@aol.com

Quantity discounts available for 10 or more copies

Thank you - for taking time - to provide feedback.
It will be helpful as I write my next book.

Thank you again and I pray that you will continue to have God's blessings.